CROSSING THE SNOWLINE

Pauline Stainer is a freelance writer and tutor. After many years in rural Essex and then on the Orkney island of Rousay, she now lives at Hadleigh in Suffolk. *Crossing the Snowline* (Bloodaxe Books, 2008) is her first new collection since *The Lady & the Hare: New & Selected Poems* (Bloodaxe Books, 2003), which drew on five previous books, as well as a new collection, *A Litany of High Waters.* Along with *The Lady & the Hare*, her collections *The Honeycomb*, *Sighting the Slave Ship* and *The Ice-Pilot Speaks* were all Poetry Book Society Recommendations. Her fourth collection *The Wound-dresser's Dream* was shortlisted for the Whitbread Poetry Award in 1996.

PAULINE STAINER

Crossing the Snowline

BLOODAXE BOOKS

821.
914
STA

ISBN: 978 1 85224 812 3

First published 2008 by
Bloodaxe Books Ltd,
Highgreen,
Tarset,
Northumberland NE48 1RP.

www.bloodaxebooks.com
For further information about Bloodaxe titles
please visit our website or write to
the above address for a catalogue.

Bloodaxe Books Ltd acknowledges
the financial assistance of
Arts Council England, North East.

Cover design: Neil Astley & Pamela Robertson-Pearce.

Printed in Great Britain by
Bell & Bain Limited, Glasgow, Scotland.

for Dickon, Simon and Ben

ACKNOWLEDGEMENTS

Acknowledgements are due to the editors of the following publications, in which some of these poems first appeared: *Poetry London*, *Poetry Review*, *The Review* and *The Warwick Review*.

'Our Lady of Indigo' was first published in *Light Unlocked*, edited by Kevin Crossley-Holland and Lawrence Sail (Enitharmon Press, 2005); 'Gift from an ebb-tide' in *The Way You Say the World*, edited by John Lucas and Matt Simpson (Shoestring Press, 2003); 'Flooding the olive-orchard', 'Borrowed Light' and 'Bystander at the visitation' in *Into the Further Reaches*, edited by Jay Ramsay (PS Avalon, 2007).

The final sequence of thirteen poems beginning with 'The Monsoon Room' was published in 2005 in limited edition by Peter Newble with illustrations by Rosamond Ulph.

CONTENTS

'Even in Siberia, there is amber'
COLIN THUBRON

'There is only one fault, incapacity to feed on light'
SIMONE WEIL

Our Lady of Indigo

Desultory blue –
the weight of water,
scarcely a blue animal
on the ark.

Blue to conjure with –
fields of blue alfalfa
making the moonlight
something else.

Profound blue –
the master of the blue crucifix
opening his throat
to her thin-blue milk.

After the Ark

How does water remain so unfamiliar?
RONI HORN

It's not told
how the animals left,
but waiting to disembark
their breath formed a cloud
and fell as light rain.

It gathered in hollows
under their eyes,
the peaceable kingdom
laid down, like memory
in a library of water

and long after landing
they would watch
for the waterspouts
and that mysterious fall
of fish from the air.

Miraculous draught of fishes

Black surgeonfish
ghost pipefish
Arabian angelfish
sabre squirrelfish
speckled sandperch
spangled emperor
eyeshadow cardinalfish
sulphur damselfish
yellowflank damselfish
whitebelly damselfish
glass fish
Egyptian starfish
redmesh starfish
crown of thorns starfish
hovering goby

The Salving

The Hindenburg
scuttled on a warm summer evening
in Scapa Flow,
perfectly upright
in seventy feet of water,
one room completely dry
after seven years
on the seabed.

What should we make of it –
this historic absence of water,
the Hindenburg
lifting, lifting
through sponges
and bluish eels
thick as a man's arm,
Jonah in the whale's belly
for three days and nights?

River landscape to Emmaus

Three men walking,
dippers working the water,
the river
writing its monograph
on mosses.

Later,
the two disciples
watch him break bread,
lightfingered,
backlit.

Not nonchalant exactly –
for love is nothing
if not improvised,
wounds troubling the light
the art of extremity.

Christ in Kashmir

It is not as we remember.
He came here
across the border
from Damascus
travelling
on a single breath.

Another of those things
which gives nothing away,
like that incident
in a forgotten garden
when the unknown young man
fled from him naked.

Indigo in Anglesey Light

Profoundly charged –
like a Chinese porcelain bowl
filling with water
until the mountain turns blue,
the sea green.

No evident magic
except that blue note –
the surfer
in his wetsuit
awaiting the seventh wave

and on the promontory
above the bruising
open water,
a moon-gazing hare
releasing the light.

Hieroglyph

The moon is pale
as a hare's belly

so what trembles
the alert stillness

of this Egyptian hare
over a ripple of water

into running script?

The shaman and his creatures

(for Elizabeth Newlands)

He gives them all
profound attention –
carnivores in their soft circle,
the owls of Nineveh
with night-vision glasses,
three hares
from the Silk Road.

Each kingdom he invokes
sounds its sonorous stone –
riderless horses
after the razing,
clouded leopards
in a garden
of perfect brightness.

Holy family with three hares

(after Dürer)

You might catch them
in a nocturnal landscape
on their flight into Egypt,
the moon dropping
thin flexible mirrors.

Or in a wild strawberry place,
wychelms coming
softly into leaf
through dispensation
of mist

the child lighter
than sugar-lift etching,
but still suckling
with the energy
of an icon.

Children of Basra

We gathered bright pieces
from the hot ground,
put them to our mouths,
metallic as blood.

Silver-tongued
the soft explosion of lesions.
the ferment of silver is silver
What is the flux for such a solder?

Dove Cottage

I wanted to weigh
Wordsworth's blue lenses
in the opium scales
left by De Quincey

his children waking
with snow on their faces
before the slates were pegged
with sheepbone

the panelling stained
with pig's blood, Dorothy
wearing her brother's ring
the night of the wedding

rushlights
burning at both ends

Monks skating

They skate on the stewpond,
their habits profoundly blue
while far below
the eels insinuate.

Clouded steel,
buds of cast silver,
Christ on the spindle tree
incarnazione.

Significant snow
has silenced all wounds,
absent objects,
compulsory figures

save forgiveness –
that moment of making
an entirely imperceptible turn
in bladed light.

The Blessing

(for Peter Johnson)

There they were –
ordinary, unknowable,
beasts waiting to be blessed
at St Luke in the Fields

some trying to break cover
as if they hear
the whizz of the biblical wind
in the mulberry trees

others, domesticated,
raising their symphony
for wild instruments
under the verve of prayer.

Over the Hudson river
the cloud puts out a paw,
skyscrapers stretch
with the heat

the bees of the invisible
are bleached in sunlight,
If anyone is in Christ
he is a new creature.

Nothing is like
the anxiety of animals
waiting for Adam
to name them

yet some lie down
in the enclosed garden
as if the tree of charity
sprang from their breasts.

Heatwave

It was August
when we saw the man
with an iguana on his shoulder
walk up from the wharf.

No mirage –
the huge lizard
unblinking
in outlandish light

while downwind
the lions at Colchester zoo
were fed lumps of ice
flavoured with blood.

John Donne in the Azores

Seven islands.
Rock, water, light
in bare-knuckled fight
at the earth's imagined corners.

Grappling irons
along the wharves,
powders
of the merchant.

It ravished him –
the quick of the place,
the hunger for
what was unmapped

birds in the wind
at dawn,
with Pentecostal tongues,
going south, going south.

The Ship's Gardener

I tend the garden on deck
while under the keel
forests of kelp
multiply.

Melons, love-apples, aubergines –
so far from land
I have to pollinate
with a paintbrush.

Exhausted birds blow in
and sip from the nectar spurs
until an archipelago
opens in their throats.

Cloudshadow on Desertas

It sulks on the horizon,
uninhabited, waterless
until the sun
red-silk sails slowly filling
slips anchor

and the moon
shafting the rockface,
allows lichens
to go on growing
with incredible slowness

up the throat of a waterfall.

Salt desert

It takes the weight out of moonlight,
this fresco washed
with quicklime,
men shovelling salt
in mask and visor.

They take the white light walk
between great crystals
edgewise,
with the glittering patience
of pack animals

while deeper
under guttered antlers,
the signatures of dark matter,
the swirling oxides
flood in.

Moonfield

This is the way
the moon revisits –
each given hour
frost-blue,
the stars blindfold

a fourfold meditation
for each quarter,
fantomqvartz
one crystal growing
inside another

until the sun,
that sometime lover,
comes up like
Christ in the Canticle
showing himself at the lattice.

Wedding Song

(for Lucy and Nick)

See them
walk the tide-line
as the oil-rig shimmers
through the fabled blue,
she, glancing up
in a gust of sunlight
like a pearl diver
opening her eyes underwater.

See them exchange
the red tabernacle
of their hearts
against a covenant
of light and water,
while dolphins sleep
on borrowed time
with one eye open.

Gift from an ebb-tide

(for Anne Stevenson, who came to Orkney)

Too isolated you said –
but I saw the island
as a word
against the whetstone
of silence

the drowned rising
as to a Bach sarabande,
intrepid, unhallowed,
while at every seventh wave
the hawk sulks.

Quandal

Clearances,
the turf
a singing green,
downwind
of the deserted crofts
an owl,
releasing its third eyelid
against the sleet,
opaque as history.

Crossing the Snowline

I still see them –
the sculptors of Kilpeck
on the road
to Santiago de Compostela,
crossing the Roman bridge
in the small hours

westward,
always westward,
Finisterre referring
its azure,
the jubilation of wolves
spilling into the cloister.

But some
never made it back
through the wilderness
to chisel
a sleeping Christ
from the living tree

and lie fallow
under their larch ceiling
as if amazed
by the irrepressible light
at the burial of the stars.

Sakurafubuki

(for Martin and Asuka)

Cherry blossom blizzard –
driven petals
in unbruised drifts.

We lie down
under their glimmering pressure
as if overwintering

hot-blooded,
open to multitude
in the spring wind.

And as we stay buried,
kimonos are laid out
high above the tree-line

spilling their scarlets
on the freshening snow.

The Source

Sculpting the Japanese dancer,
he felt the gliding phases
by which girl became bird

the lost-wax feathering
of her breast, her hair
swept back in a molten comb.

But what finally held him
as he broke the mould,
was how a casting-seam

gave her body
its chance translation.

Michelangelo's snowman

It stands there
solid with moonlight
in the piazza,
commissioned by the Medicis
after unseasonable snow.

No image survives,
despite instruments
so sensitive they can measure
the depression of snowfall
on the earth.

But it still burns
naked, unmelting
between memory and event
as if the heart had
condensed through the breast.

The Flaying of Marsyas
(after Titian)

Who would have guessed this
a holy technique?
Michelangelo perhaps,
carrying his own flayed skin
into the Last Judgement.

Dante invoked Apollo
to embody Paradise,
but here the kneeling god
flays the living
for a lapdog.

Ecstasy
strips to the quick :
the suspended satyr
sheds his senses
with eyes wide-open.

Cool inspiriting,
when poets hear
the cuckoo call
as soldiers die
in one another's arms.

The red and the white

It's the blanching season,
each tree
a small crucifixion
in winter light.

So many sites for bloodletting,
sepia, sanguine, black,
a white-breasted hawk
snow-lit

calves exposing their throats
in the slipstream
of the cattle-truck
while watching for the morning.

Madonna lilies

Their fluted whites
should rebuke all fever

but they thirst, they thirst,
tongues urgent with pollen

for the angel's transaction,
the accidents of bread and wine.

After Vermeer

A girl reading
at an open window,
the fugitive blues
so close they kiss.

Outside, the pressure
of sap in sunlight,
tulips, upbeat
on ground of vermilion.

Lady with a squirrel
(after Holbein)

He painted simply
her awareness of being painted

but we, who must make
things happen

see the silver leash
race through her fingers

the squirrel's reflex,
grace of electrons.

Inhabiting the high wire

(after Philippe Petit)

When I walk
the glass pavilions,
the crowd, looking up
through the cavalletti,
see a daylight moon
suspended on gimbals.

Is gravity what it was?
Under the spires
of St John the Divine,
I knelt on the wire
barefoot, or in ballet slippers,
with an eighteen foot pole.

Over the canyon,
I will lie on the cable
listening
to taped music
and temporise

like a particle of light
playing in two places
at once
without crossing any space
in between.

After the tsunami

There are dunes here now
and new hives,
bees in upper and lower rooms
feeling vibration
through the soles of their feet.

But this moment of equilibrium –
a contortionist
balancing glasses of wine
on her diaphragm
to the sound of the celeste

how shall we hold it,
when so many things go missing
and the living are rolled below
as if death were
spherical?

Retribution

Eel-grass,
the wind in the reeds
saying the unsayable.

Was it what we heard
or what we thought
we heard?

One thing for certain –
when water moves
through land

the world is hung
on nothing.

After Cimabue

November floods
have ravaged Florence.
In the refectory of Santa Croce
Christ who walked on the water
drowns on the cross.

The morticians
have made an inventory
of the divine body

inspected lesions
on poplar, canvas, gesso,
dismantled the halo's disc

held sampling-flasks
to underglaze bleeding,
glimpsed fungal spores on the skin

grafted the flesh
from the primed ground
as if disembodiment were an art.

Who is it waits
at a solemn distance
leaning against the piers,
a divining-crystal in each eye?

It is Dante,
deep in his native Arno,
the river rising
through his shade

clouding
as with blood
the residual beauty
of the heart's image.

Dante at the Three Gorges

I saw him
on the dam-wall
above the Yangtze

to his left,
steeljaws crushing the granite
into every conceivable size of grit

to his right,
men sweeping the dust
with bundles of willow

at his back
twenty-five thousand workers
surfacing from their drowned valley.

And suddenly he was gone –
walking the ten shiplocks
like a Jesus lizard

while far below
ancestral sturgeon
waited for the earthquake.

Iwaishima

On this island
only the dead look simultaneously
east and west.

There's the rustle of bamboo,
a lizard in the stepped-field,
unharvested rice.

The old wear bonnets against sun and salt,
load little cable-cars
with loquats, oranges.

When the priest left,
abalone fishers drew up nothing
but a blue risk of thunder.

In the empty school
children lay fingers to our lips
until we who linger

can only weigh their unwritten lives
against the hidden messages
in water.

Five haiku from the island

Night overdyed,
the souls of ancestors
a candle between mirrors

Buzzard
master of blue inscription
complicit in the haze

Drowned cargoes of cobalt
and pearl, hearsay
or the speech of birds?

Near distance,
jacks, yellowtails, half-beaks
at a shining remove

Rising azure.
When the dead are blue
is it cold or remorse?

About Suffering

Kafka could make it
contrapuntal,
but what did Liszt hear
when he saw Paganini
at the Paris Opera,
the prescribed mercury
rotting his lower jaw?

Unplayed music –
pall-bearers
wading the night waves
with his unshriven body,
that cadenza
which leaves no visible wake
on the heart.

The Seaward Window
(for Gill and Jon Haylett)

Sunlight in a blue room,
the sea beyond.
Nothing to kindle the glass
except a skein of geese
crossing the sound,
and that deep arrow,
atavistic, oneiric,
as they cut the blue
above the red undertow.

Swans alighting

December,
the solstice on its hinge
of salt and fire.

When the swans flew down
we lost them
in the dazzle.

Yet I remember
their erasure
by the burning water

as if things
in the darkness of light
are made whole.

Epiphany Eve

The meths-drinkers
have bared their chests,
taken flame-water
to escape the gravity
of the flesh,
yet even they stop singing
when the swans fly over.

The night is pounced with gold.
The meths-drinkers
have taken out their eyes
but still see
the breasts of bodies
grown so cold
they no longer shine.

Quaker burial

It is halfway through Lent –
no rubrics,
books of hours,
music or liturgy

simply the dead
unlearning the light
between greenish schists
while the moon mines its cobalt.

Border-crossing

Don't look back.
The dead thrum
through the marram grass
in search of a voice.

Follow
this laying fallow,
an iron earth
burning its thistles.

Not exile
but overwintering,
dumb light
on dead wood

coming at equinox
out of darkness
and in silence,
for want of a better word.

Long-barrow

Silence listens to itself here,
but we are still undone
by the way the dead
disburden.

Put your ear
to the organised dust,
grave-goods
for improbable journeys

a bird singing
of time out,
down holloways
of bone.

Drovers

They came down holloways
between blue sloes.

I have come to know
that register of blue-darks

juniper berries deepening
through woodsmoke

the pungency of bruised herbs
at dusk

slow-burn
of driven beasts

blue intake of breath
at pasture beyond.

Seahenge

It is April –
a moon ripples
the sea sunwards,
the great oak hauled
on ropes of plaited honeysuckle
into its salt circle.

But memory is more pliant
than time –
those rings of sapwood
still harden into heartwood
as if the dead are
spoken for.

Words

accrue marvellous blemishes,
glassbones disease
Ostogenesis Imperfecta

surface like seals
after great distances,
equilibrists of otherness

blood-irons wrapped in silk,
allowing mysterious little
haemorrhages

sparrow-hawks
thrown in the hunt,
oxen of the sun.

Yarnwinder

From the air
they look like half-tone tattoos -
elongated trapezoid,
double spiral into zigzag,
pattern of yarn and needle
three thousand feet long.

No sign of rain –
but when the sun
rattles its cage
the sand particles sigh
in the sudden change
like silkworms
spinning their shroud.

Solstice bird

Nasca – an adze of blue
against the gorget
of the humming bird.

They gather nectar
and pollinate
at the same time

their breasts refracting
the red updraught
where the dead lie

lips sealed
with a thorn, along
the moonrise line.

Conjunctions

You lay with me in the bleached field,
new moon, late sun

they hung like counterweights,
first light, last light

no orient, except to kiss and graze
as if each moment were an open wound

and when we separate, only heart's spectra
indexing the dark.

The Borrowdyke

We stood between waters
on the black fen

blocks of raw glass
running bright-blue

pure horizontals
perilous with hawthorn

a single swan offset
against the dropping dusk

as if all perfected things
are lonely.

Rising marsh

Managed retreat,
men reflooding the marshes,
decoy ponds
with their rustle
of silver-phased eels
smelling the sea.

A drover's enclosure
where sheep browse
in their salt aureole,
and that subtler
vanishing-point –
a centurion's ghost
wading old damson hedges
up to the knee.

Cobra Mist, Orford Ness

It could be a focus for meditation –
the concrete circle
and radar masts.

You might even feel
attuned to these antennae
of twilight.

Nothing vivid or overblown
until beyond the saltings
foxes raze the electric field

with their burning tails.

Water-spiral

Time and space
come together
in the Islamic garden,
the soul
recognising itself
as living water.

It is all in the beholding –
overhead
a light aircraft
on delicate manoeuvres
climbs seven spirals
to the summit.

Flooding the olive orchard

We hardly noticed it –
water rising in the grass,
a silent flooding in sunlight.

Not memory but revision;
time waylaid
by things that never surface

olives throwing back their silver,
bees drinking
the enlightened water.

The Sifting

Silt-roddens,
medieval watercourses
newly ploughed
across the fen.

Things work to the surface.
Five wits
from lesser graves,
unrealised script

the middle island
gone in a flicker,
knucklebones still whitening
while fighting their corner.

The Whitening

Seven kings
stir under the chalk quarry
white-fleshed as eels.

Which blizzard
they will ride through
before scouring the turf

I do not know –
blackthorn whitening the wind,
fossil dust rising

but when they emerge
from muffled detonations
into a milky sun

each horse and rider
will be whiter
than the nests of cave-swifts

made from saliva.

Dowland at Elsinore

Nowhere, as resident musician,
can he escape
the pinch of isolation,
snow falling without wind
down the corridors of power

the leaves dropping
as if shriven,
his passionate pavanes
absorbing all light
except blue

a moon rising
ungirdled.

Mozart at the Falconry Lodge, 1763

What did he hear
when he saw the peregrines
with eyelids sewn together,
each eye weighing
more than an ounce,
larger and heavier than his own?

A cargo of hawkbells,
or the larynx of a bird outside
igniting silk sky
and sloe-blossom,
like his own tame starling
whistling its fantasia
for mechanical organ?

The Raven Master

Young ravens
in the White Tower,
cross-lit, conspiratorial.

He is teaching them to talk –
calls them
an unkindness of seven

as if remembering
their prophetic tongues
leading wolves to prey

the deer stepping
through tall blue mist
to water unseen

the speech of birds
picking memory clean.

Deer coming to water unseen

When will they break cover
in that long minute
between the jumping hours,
mist burning off their bellies
as they crash
through the underbrush?

I wait for it —
the running of the deer
on an altered gradient,
not the scent of water
but an older thirst,
the hart desiring the waterbrooks.

The flowers of persuasion

I had been looking for a different light –
not the yellow gloom
of rapefields ripening in rain

nor the window-cleaner
refloating the sun
from his cradle against the smoke-glass

but the blue hare
loping through pollen-light
in praise of the horizon.

The Dancing Field

This is the history of light

barley tinged with purple
under plover's-egg blue

scintillation of mirrors
to allure larks

pale-clouded yellows
lifting under a hunter's moon

leverets with large hearts
in the liquid grass

the lovely litany of field names
guarding the flame.

A Pouch of Saffron

It is October.
Beyond the saffron field
orange poplars
talk in tongues.

When the dew has dried,
saffron-gatherers
nip the purple blooms
at the base

giddy with
barbarous blood-sugars,
the pressure of sunlight
on pistil and stamen

floating sleeves
of gossamer
from their wicker baskets
still telling the yellow.

Spinsters

(for Judy White)

It wears fingers to the bone,
spinning a sullen thread
while the sun spins straw into gold.

And Mary –
was she spinning, her sleeves
catching the spittle of the sun

when the angel appeared
in his notoriously fugitive yellows
over the wheel of the horizon?

Voltage

Wet streets,
shining slates,
indigo on a tremble
as if dew
is wrung from it,
the mistle thrushes
of Paradise Street
nesting in January
on a lamp-post
in Liverpool.

Casual, particular,
as when Mary
in electric blue
before the angel,
kept the place
in the book she was reading
with her left thumb.

Bystander at the visitation

I first saw them
as figures without a context –
but as they embraced
in the silence
between one utterance
and another

I glimpsed
Mary and Elisabeth,
the action of sunlight
on dew,
their unborn children,
innocent of syntax

listening in.

Mantegna's Hares

We looked out –
the weather whistle-blue,
hares running with the wind
above water where
the sun never reaches.

Give me
the pulse of a hare,
that zigzag between
breath and the moment –
Mantegna's hares, still boxing
beside the agony in the garden.

Borrowed Light

Three Maries at the sepulchre –
insolent light
on a blue lintel.

No soft focus –
chemical messengers
have silica in their wings

the hot specifics
from some occurrence
outside the picture

a tree
in quiet landscape
becoming radiant.

Afterlight

(for my daughter)

I chose the liquidambar tree
knowing it would light
its own dying,
like those wasted children
wrapped in gold foil
to keep them warm.

Each autumn
when leaves fall
with the first frost
not even the kings of Persia
wore such saffron-yellow shoes
across the glimmering fallow.

I use them –
the colours of grief,
like the mirror
in the cat's eye
to throw back
the single topaz at your throat.

The Apple House

The apples are fat
with solitude and light,
they take over the room
without echo.

Pale cattle
feeding from pale hay
in the lifting mist
do not look up.

This is the least shared
of all spaces,
the light lying fallow,
the apples ripening.

The Monsoon Room

The pavilion should be fragrant
with dripping curtains
of Indian rush,
but under the painted clouds
multiple mirrors
ask questions about rain.

The indigo vats sulk.
Let us feed the serpent with milk
until the blue he withholds
in his manifold hood
rubs off on the skin
and can be burnished.

Let us dream
of an alcove blue
with smoke from the ghats,
of rain coming
so delicately scored
it is entirely *rubato*.

The Convoy

Not the profound machinery
of gods,
but military vehicles
coming from great distance,
headlights scenting
the sandstorm.

A more intense country –
the light dropping its guard
on the great dust
of the world,
sandvipers
in their hot yellows

and beyond,
as if there were no
rules of engagement,
racks of new-dyed sarees
billowing
the scarlet wind.

The Drum House

So many overtones –
Honeycomb hanging
from a parapet
below the palace drums,
timbre between the two.

Indian swifts
coming back on themselves
as echo and re-echo
at the wide, latticed windows,
never alighting.

Green parakeets
so shrill they could
dispirit any drum,
vibration
charming the snake

infra-red
and indigo answer,
that light notation
between a noon drum
and the last silence.

The Day Bed

She is her own island,
half-sleep
a fugue in two colours
on the coils
of the many-headed serpent.

Only firecrackers
alter the dream.
From the city below
winds trade in indigo
through a market of spare parts

and beyond streetsleepers
at the palace gate,
she hears bamboo wands
whip an early dew
from the scalding grass.

The Queen's Bangle-maker

Manifold bangles –
malachite,
mottled agate,
lapis lazuli.
He has made them all.

But the ones
he slips over her wrist –
queen's blue,
garter blue,
milk blue –
ripple with
a glass-blower's breath
about the bone

and when he has gone,
she takes up
the secret mirror with yellow birds,
the coiled opiates,
the little antelope.

Ghost Writers to the Emperor

They still inhabit language,
caught between the unsaid
and the unsayable,
hands dappled as apricots
in the latticed light

making their mark
like elephants at a salt-lick,
until only the text
and its inspired omissions
risk the silence.

Chattris

Mausoleums lying
in the lee of the wind turbines,
electricity
between act and essence.

Which is the subtler body –
the blacksmith's wife
veiled in yellow
pumping the muslin bellows

or the concubine
burning in her separate fire
with handprints
of vermilion?

The Astrologer's Seat

A pavilion of sandstone
newly chiselled.
Horoscopes
cast from the exact moment
of birth,
drought encroaching.

Nothing to slake
any fix on the stars
except the unforeseen
conjunction
of dumb planets
and the word for water.

Desert Fox

outrunning the sand-ripple,
insolent as light

dew on his breast
of burnt-in colours

narrative of fire
from brush and underbelly

dazzle-camouflage
as he crosses frontiers.

Sun Prayers

Swing your diadem.
Only Vishnu's head
cut by the bowstring
troubles the light.

Soften the rock.
Release slow fireballs
of honey
for the bee-eater.

Stand still.
Give the rows of cymbals
shining on their racks
a day to cool down.

Keep from us
that secret alloy
which prevents the cymbal
from shattering.

Let exposure
at high noon
be a canticle
of suspended dew.

Drop your yellow
and red underwings.
As we cross the void
overshadow us.

Jantar manta

A drummer climbs
to the top of the gnomen,
beats each hour
and half-hour
for successive maharajahs.

Why keep time
when the same word
is used for yesterday
as for tomorrow?

What I hear
are the unstruck hours
of standard time,
settling like a blizzard
on these solids and voids
in the sun
while the stars kneel
unbewildered
on their blue lintel.

Water Buffalo

There they were –
dividing
the green-mantled waters,
a widening wake
at their back
going blackly
into the middle distance.

What was it –
that momentum
between image and reflection,
the way they re-wrote
the black on the green
by wading the sky
with no shadow of turning?

The Ferry

Did the shore-line
alter with the dawn
as we sculled
to the sandstone pagoda?

Memory still throws
its quoit of polished steel
over that crossing
by water

for how could we
judge distance
in the haze of firecrackers
after Divali

mist rising
from a river
slow with garlands
of marigolds?

Yet we sat there
like those people
in dreams
who never speak up

but who go
lightly and swiftly
without any error
to some imperious shore.